Sometimes I Like to Fight, But I Don't Do It Much Anymore

By Lawrence E. Shapiro, Ph.D.
Illustrated by Timothy Parrotte
Designed by Charles Brenna

Published by:
The Center for Applied Psychology, Inc.
P.O. Box 1587, King of Prussia, PA 19406 U.S.A.
Tel. 1-800-962-1141

The Center for Applied Psychology, Inc. is Publisher of Childswork/Childsplay, a catalog of products for mental health professionals, teachers and parents a who wish to help children with their social and emotional growth needs.

ISBN 1-82732-22-7

Sometimes I Like to Fight, But I Don't Do It Much Anymore

A Self-Esteem Book for Children with Difficulty in Controlling Their Anger

By Lawrence E. Shapiro, Ph.D.

Illustrated by Timothy Parrotte

The Center for Applied Psychology, Inc.
King of Prussia, PA

Other Books by Lawrence E. Shapiro, Ph.D.

Play-and-Read series books
ALL FEELINGS ARE OK -ITS WHAT YOU DO WITH THEM THAT COUNTS
FACE YOUR FEELINGS
TAKE A DEEP BREATH: THE KIDS PLAY-AWAY STRESS BOOK
HOW TO BE A SUPER-HERO

Self-Esteem Series Books
SOMETIMES I DRIVE MY MOM CRAZY, BUT I KNOW SHE'S CRAZY ABOUT ME
THE BUILDING BLOCKS OF SELF-ESTEEM: A Skill-Oriented Approach to Teaching Self-Worth
THE VERY ANGRY DAY AMY DIDN'T HAVE
JUMPIN' JAKE SETTLES DOWN

Reference Books
THE BOOK OF PSYCHOTHERAPEUTIC GAMES
CHILD THERAPY TODAY
SHORT-TERM THERAPY WITH CHILDREN
FORMS FOR USE IN COUNSELING CHILDREN
TRICKS OF THE TRADE: 101 TECHNIQUES TO HELP CHILDREN CHANGE

There are many explanations of why excessive fighting and aggression seems to be so common in today's children. Some blame it on the increased stresses that children experience and specifically on the breakdown of the traditional family structure. Others point at the increase in violence on TV and the proliferation of aggressive toys. Still others might fault society's misplaced values or concerns. Whatever the causes, excessive fighting and aggression in school-age children must be dealt with appropriately and effectively.

This book is designed to be read to children by caring adults, who will hopefully use it as a jumping-off point for interventions which will lead to behavioral change. In hearing and discussing the story of a child who learns to overcome and control his aggressiveness, children may be more motivated and cooperative in finding solutions to their own behavioral problems.

It is also hoped that the protagonist in this book will be a "role-model" for the aggressive child. The "hero" of the book, Douglas, learns to accept help from others and find that while change is not quick, or easy, it is worthwhile. The positive relationships that Douglas develops are at least as important as his behavioral change.

At the end of this book, the techniques used with Douglas are reviewed to help you implement them for a child you know who "sometimes" likes to fight.

-Lawrence E. Shapiro, Ph.D.

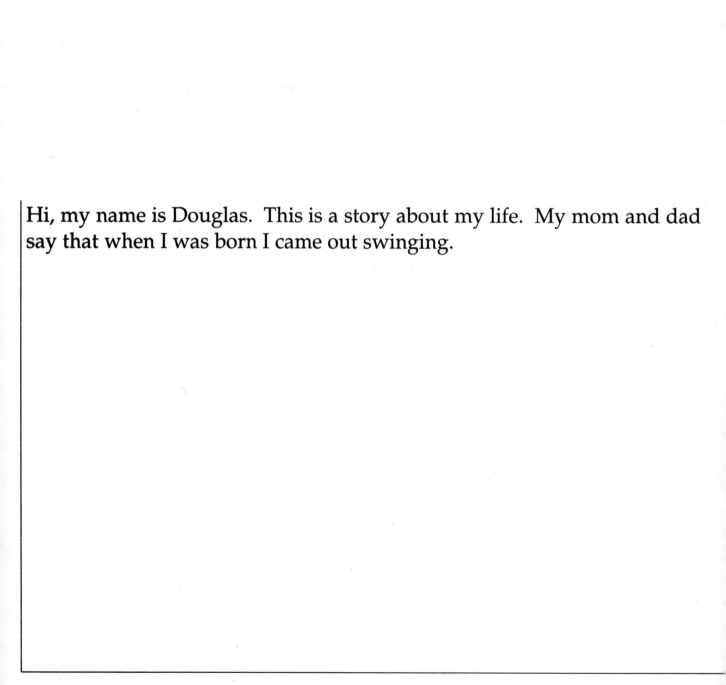

Hi, my name is Douglas. This is a story about my life. My mom and dad say that when I was born I came out swinging.

When I was little, I liked to wrestle with my Dad. And I was so strong that sometimes I beat him up!

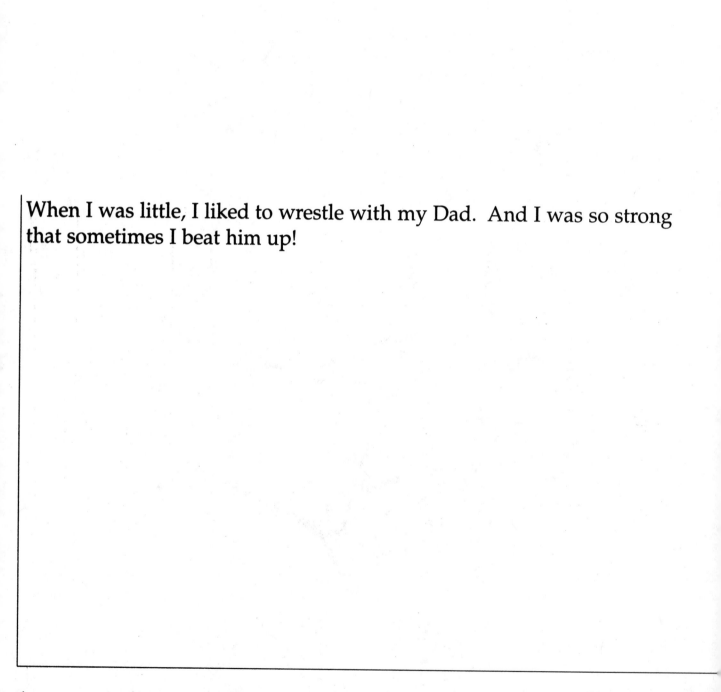

I have an older brother Pete who used to fight with me, too (until Mom said that we had to stop).

We used to fight all the time . . .

Pillow fights.
Water gun fights.
Wrestling fights.
Sword fights.
Gun fights.

It was fun. . .

But one time, Pete twisted my arm, and I hit him, and then he pulled my fingers back real hard and I had to go to the hospital.

11

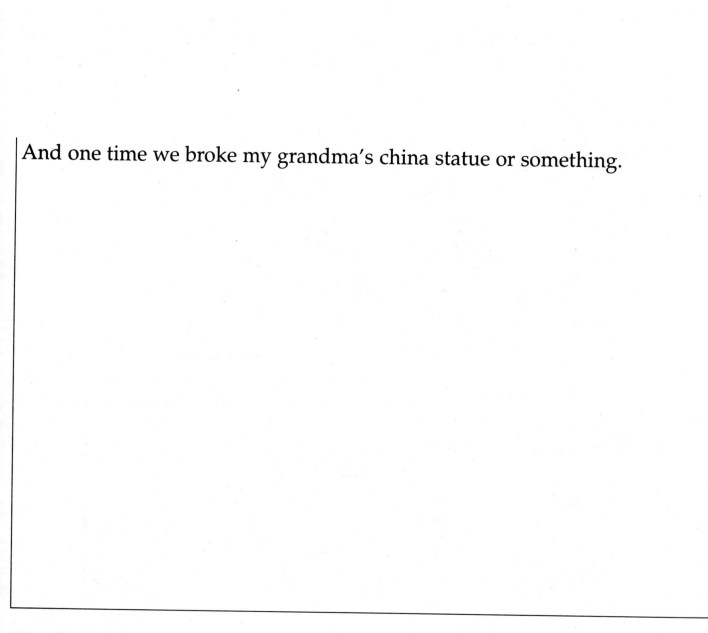

And one time we broke my grandma's china statue or something.

And another time we were fighting in the hardware store and the man behind the counter said we had to leave, because we were going to hurt somebody.

And so my mom and dad had a meeting with us and said that we couldn't fight anymore, and that we would be in a lot of trouble if we did. And they said that Pete was much older, so it was up to him to stop fighting and then he stopped playing with me altogether!

Then it seemed like no one liked anything I did . . . ever!

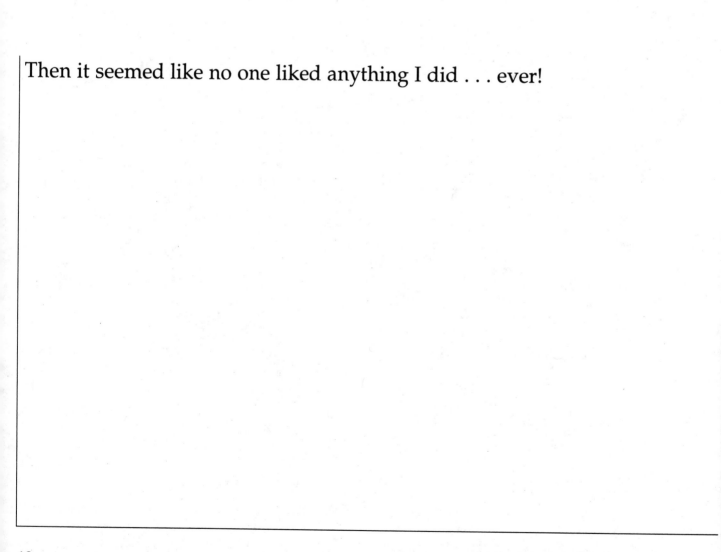

When it was Halloween, I wanted to be a pirate, but my teacher said I couldn't. So I went as a stupid clown and the kids laughed at me and teased me.

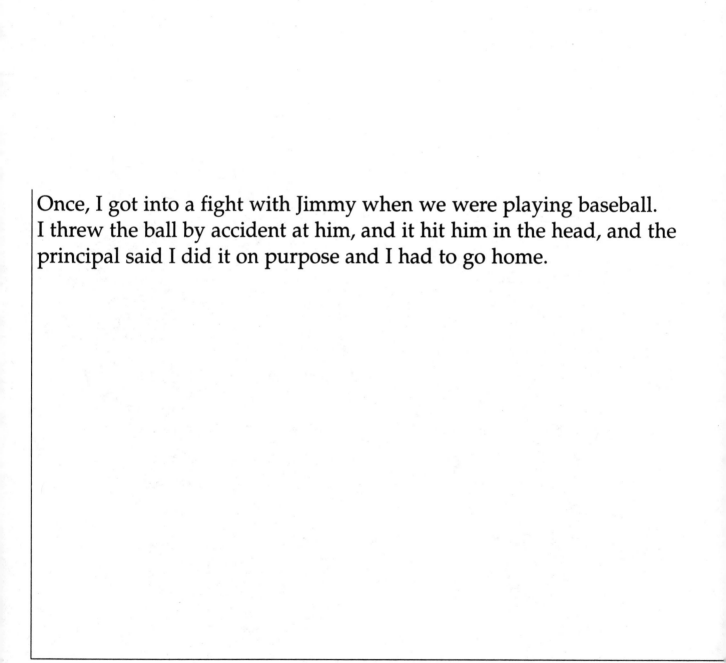

Once, I got into a fight with Jimmy when we were playing baseball. I threw the ball by accident at him, and it hit him in the head, and the principal said I did it on purpose and I had to go home.

And then my teacher said I couldn't sit next to any of the boys in class, because I couldn't keep my hands to myself, and she made me sit with the girls, and they hated me.

Even when I was home and playing with my action figures, my mom said that all I did was fight and "play" fight, and she was going to take all my guys away!

Then I was mad at everyone! My mom and dad were mean. My teacher was mean. All the kids at school hated me. No one wanted to be my friend.

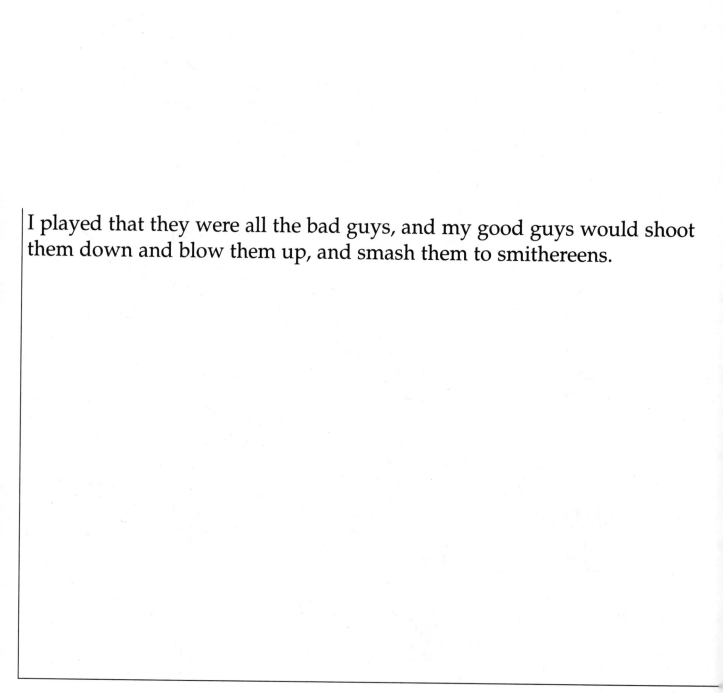

I played that they were all the bad guys, and my good guys would shoot them down and blow them up, and smash them to smithereens.

Then one day, my mom told me to come over to the couch and she looked very sad. I thought that something bad had happened, like when Grandpa died, but she said that nothing like that had happened.

"I'm just sad because you seem so unhappy all the time."

"You never hug me anymore. You don't seem to want to talk to me or Dad anymore. Your grades aren't very good, and your teacher says that you don't try very hard at school and that you act like you don't want to be there."

"Your teacher told me that there's a person at school, a counselor, who talks to kids who are unhappy, and I said that it was okay for you see her."

I didn't say anything, because I didn't have anything to say. But I thought, "Oh, great. I know that stupid counselor at school, Ms. Pincus. All the bad kids and the stupid kids go to see her and she sticks pins in them or something."

"And I'm going to see her, too," my mom said, but I wasn't really listening anymore.

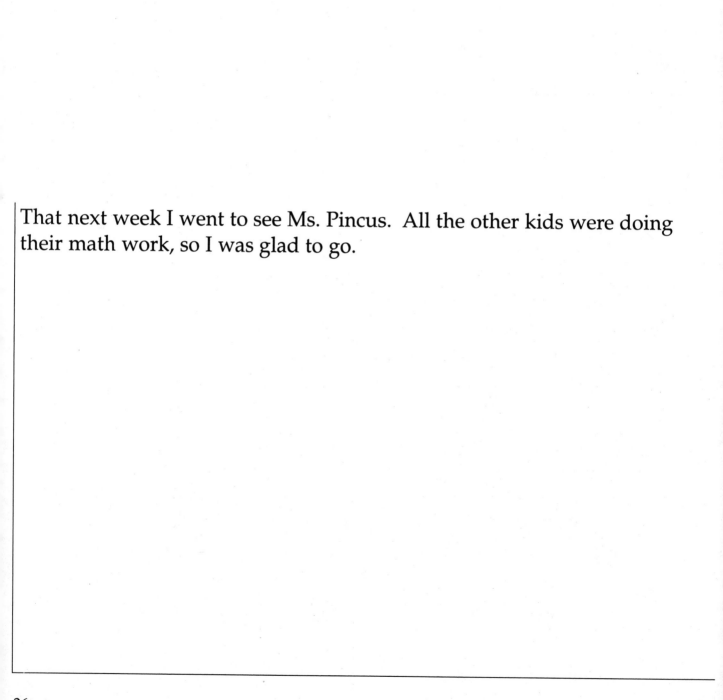

That next week I went to see Ms. Pincus. All the other kids were doing their math work, so I was glad to go.

When I walked into Ms. Pincus's room, I thought I was in the wrong place. She didn't look mean; she looked pretty nice. And she had a lot of toys and games on her bookshelf.

She told me to sit down on a chair.

"I understand that you're having a problem getting along with other people," she said.

I didn't say anything.

"Well, I've seen a lot of children like you! Your mom and your teacher have also told me that you're mad about things all the time and that you get into trouble on the playground. Those are things I think I can help you with, too." Then Mrs. P. asked me if I wanted to play some game that she had, and so we did, and she talked to me about some stuff, like why I didn't like school and what I did when I was at home.

I met with Ms. P. a few times by myself. (She said I could call her Ms. P., so I did.) We played games and we talked mostly, and I guess she was pretty nice to me.

She told me that she met with my mom and my teacher, too. I thought that they were all going to gang up on me. Or send me away. Or lock me in a closet. Or take away all my toys.

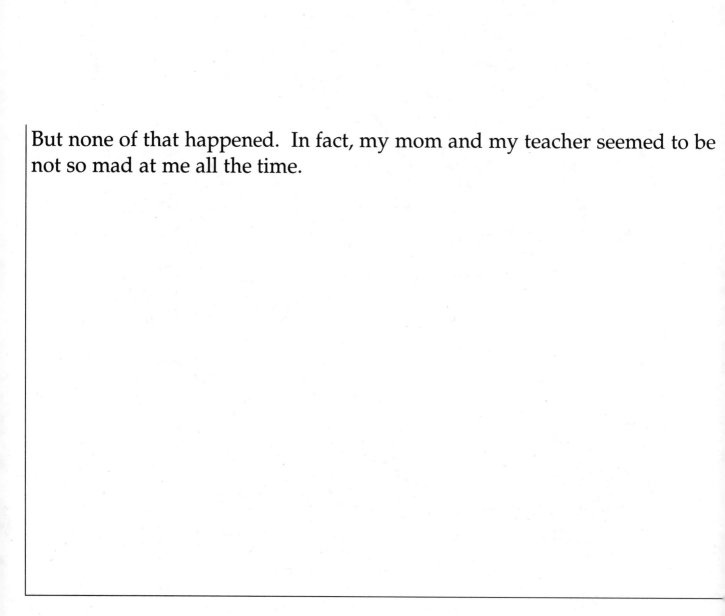

But none of that happened. In fact, my mom and my teacher seemed to be not so mad at me all the time.

And then I noticed that other things started to change.

My mom and dad started to play with me more.

On Mondays, Wednesdays, and Fridays, Mom would play with me. And on Tuesdays, Thursdays, and Saturdays, Dad would play.

They said we would play for fifteen minutes each day, and that we could play with anything I wanted, even action figures. Mom called it "Special Time."

At school, Ms. P. formed a club—The Friends Club.

We met every week, three other boys and one girl. We talked about stuff that we didn't like, and we played sometimes, and sometimes we made stuff. Ms. P. said that it was good to talk about feelings and learn about other people's feelings, so we played a game called Feelings Charades, which was fun.

Ms. Pincus said that we could talk about <u>anything</u> that we wanted to at the Friends Club.

Sometimes we hit a big pillow and called it names, which was funny. Ms. P. said that if we were mad we could hit pillows and things like that, but not people or animals. Ms. P. said to hit the pillow while we thought of the Mad Monster. She said that the Mad Monster made kids angry at the wrong times and at the wrong things. Ms. P. said to get mad at the Mad Monster rather than at the people who were trying to help us.

Sometimes we played a game called The Problem Solving Game, where we learned to think about things before we did them.

Like if Billy teased me on the playground, I used to fight with him. But then I said to myself, "What else can I do besides fight him?"

I could: Ignore him.
Tell the teacher.
Count to 10.

Then I decided to just ignore him, and he stopped bothering me.

One thing that I didn't like, but then I got used to, was not watching TV and playing video games so much.

Mom said that I had to be on a TV diet. She said that kids watch too much TV, particularly TV that is bad for you.

She said that I could only spend 10 hours a week watching TV and playing video games!

At first I was really mad at that.

I said things like:

"I hate TV.
I hate you.
I don't care if I ever watch TV again.
This is stupid.
I'm not going to school anymore. I'm not doing anything!"

But then Mom and Dad sat down with me and made a list of the shows that I could watch. And most of the ones I like, I can still watch.

Then they said that they would find other things that I could do instead of watching TV, like hobbies and stuff.

My teacher gave me a special chart to use at school.

When I had a good class period, I got a sticker on my chart.

When I got all the stickers for a day, my teacher would give me a PERFECT DAY CERTIFICATE. When I got 10 stickers, I got to choose from a box of prizes that Ms. P. kept in her room.

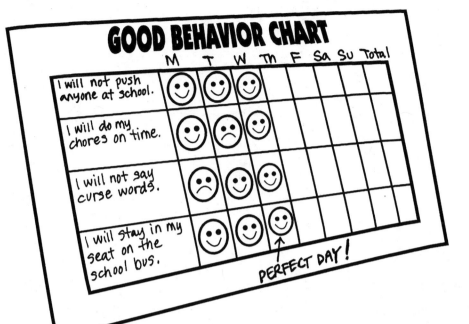

GOOD BEHAVIOR CHART

	M	T	W	Th	F	Sa	Su	Total
I will not push anyone at school.	😊	😊	😊					
I will do my chores on time.	😊	🙁	😊					
I will not say curse words.		😕	😊	😊				
I will stay in my seat on the school bus.	😊	😊	😊					

PERFECT DAY!

THIS IS TO PRESENT THAT DOUGLAS HAS HAD A PERFECT DAY!

Now it's almost the end of school. Everyone says I did a really great job this year, and Mom and Dad told me that I could take a camping trip this summer as a reward.

I think I might bring some of my soldiers on the trip. I still like to fight with them and Mom says it's okay, because I have a better "attitude." I don't know. I just thought they might need a vacation, too.

Techniques To Help Children Control Their Fighting

Most programs designed to help aggressive children involve the combination of techniques, which are implemented in the home and the school, as well as in the counseling office. Sometimes one or two techniques will be enough, and yet it is difficult to know exactly which techniques children will respond to before they have actually been tried. Reading *Sometimes I Like To Fight* with children, as a prelude to interventions, will help the professional or parent introduce techniques in a non-threatening way, and will provide a way for many children to participate in the planning of their own intervention program.

p. 44 Special Time

The counselor recommends that each parent spend fifteen minutes a day playing with Douglas. This intervention is called "Special Time," and is one of the simplest and most important techniques that can be used to help children with behavioral problems. The parent simply commits to doing anything that the child wants for a short period of time, everyday, as long as it has no associated cost and the activity is safe. This fifteen minutes symbolizes the "unconditional" love and acceptance that all children need, but children with behavioral problems rarely experience. No matter what the child has done that day, the parent still spends Special Time with the child, which consists of the *uncritical* and *non-judgmental* sharing of activities. Sometimes parents have a difficult time being uncritical, particularly when the child has had a bad day. Special Time will only be effective, however, if the parent enters into the activity with the right attitude. During Special Time, parents are in effect acting as co-therapists and should be helped to understand how this time will build self-esteem within the child and create a stronger parent-child bond.

p. 45 Doll Play

During Special Time, Douglas has chosen to play with his action figures. While many people feel that "war toys" and "action figures" encourage aggressive play and fighting, this type of play can also be looked at as a type of "therapeutic doll play." Parents can be taught how to "role play" using the child's action figures, encouraging the verbalization of feelings, problem-solving, and appropriate conflict resolution.

p. 46 The Friends Club

Small groups are an excellent way for aggressive children to learn more appropriate social skills. For many aggressive children, it is the only positive experience they have with children their own age. Groups should meet regularly and for at least 10 sessions to allow for positive relationships to be established. Typically groups for angry and aggressive children use activities as a stimulus for learning self-control and helping children verbalize their feelings.

p. 46 Feelings Charades

There are many games that can help children learn to express their feelings and understand the feelings of others. Feelings Charades is a simple game that children enjoy. It is designed to help them both express feelings and "read" the ways that people express feelings non-verbally. To play, take 20 index cards and write a "feelings word" on each card (e.g. mad, sad, glad, guilty, afraid, etc.). Then have each child, in turn, pick a card and act out that feeling without using any words. The other players have one minute to guess that feeling. The person who guesses correctly gets one point, and the player who is acting-out the feeling gets one point. Then they must each tell of a time that they had that feeling to get a second point. The person with the most points at the end of 15 minutes is the winner.

p. 48 The Mad Monster Game (Hitting A Pillow)

There is considerable controversy over whether teaching an aggressive child to hit a pillow or other soft object helps them learn to control their aggression or actually encourages it. The assumption behind this technique is that children can learn to displace their anger and discharge their energy in a safe way. In the Mad Monster Game, the children are also taught a cognitive technique: to see their anger as separate from themselves, a "monster" that gets them into trouble. Externalizing the problem motivates many children to plan and carry out a strategy to conquer their behavioral problem.

p. 50 The Problem-Solving Game
Problem-solving training seems to be an effective way for many children to learn alternatives to acting-out their feelings. In problem-solving training, children are taught to: identify situations where they are likely to act aggressively; find behavioral alternatives which inhibit the aggression (like counting to 10); find cognitive alternatives (thinking about other things they could do); weigh the various alternatives; and then practice the alternative they have chosen. To play the "game," have the children make up scenarios similar to the real life situations in which they act aggressively. Write them on index cards, and then have a "leader" pick one of the cards at random. The leader should direct the other children in acting the problem out and practicing the problem-solving technique.

p. 52 The TV Diet
Nearly any teacher of young children will tell you how much "aggressive" TV shows and video games contribute to actual fighting behavior. Perhaps more importantly, the average American child spends 24-hours a week in front of the TV—a day a week—and few will argue that this is time well spent. Rather than watching TV, children can benefit from spending more time in creative play, playing sports, exploring hobbies, and so on. Most children will more readily accept a TV diet when structured and fun activities are there to take the place of TV.

p. 58 Behavioral Charts and Contracts
Behavioral charts and contracts are almost always one of the most effective tools that can be used with behavioral problems. Although critics of these techniques say that they don't teach children internal controls, they usually do result in quick behavioral change and can result in better peer relations, more approval by adults, and a subsequent increase in self-worth. When using behavioral programs, care should be taken to follow behavioral principles: be realistic in setting goals; be consistent in giving points or taking them away; use rewards which are motivating to the child; follow-through on consequences.

ORDER THESE OTHER THERAPEUTIC STORY BOOKS
AND ACTIVITY BOOKS BY DR. SHAPIRO

Sometimes I Drive My Mom Crazy, But I Know She's Crazy About Me

This warm, humorous, and true-to-life story of a young AD/HD boy addresses the many difficult and frustrating issues that kids like him confront everyday—from sitting still in the classroom, to remaining calm, to feeling "different" from other children. This book is an amusing look at how this youngster develops a sense of self-worth by learning to deal with his problems with the help of the adults who care about him. Hailed by parents and educators as one of the best books written to help motivate AD/HD children to cope with their problem in a positive way. Paperback. Ages 6-12.

The Very Angry Day That Amy Didn't Have

Margaret and Amy are two girls in the same class who coincidentally are both having a very difficult day. But Margaret always makes things worse by her negative reactions, making people mad at her, while Amy finds positive ways to solve the various problems she encounters. This simple but poignant book is an excellent tool to help young children learn alternatives to getting angry. Paperback. For ages 4-10.

Jumpin' Jake Settles Down: A Workbook to Help Impulsive Children Learn to Think Before They Act

This hilariously-illustrated story and activity book tells how Jake changes from an itchin-kind-of-frog to a responsible thinkin'-kind-of-frog. The book features 50 activities that help children learn cognitive techniques and behavioral skills to control their impulsivity. Paperback. For ages 5-10.

Face Your Feelings

This book includes 52 pictures of children, teens, adults, and older adults, expressing the feelings that children are most concerned about. With each picture, the person tells about the kinds of things that made him/her feel that way. Includes a mylar mirror to help children "face their own feelings." Paperback. Ages 3 and up.

The Building Blocks of Self-Esteem

Self-esteem is more than just self-love. It's a deep sense of self-worth based on the mastery of specific traits and skills which help children succeed and develop positive relationships with others. This workbook is filled with activities that form a multi-modal approach to improving a child's self-esteem: Affect, Behavior, Cognition, Developmental, Education, Social System. Paperback. Ages 5-12.

TO ORDER, OR FOR A FREE CATALOG OF BOOKS AND GAMES THAT ADDRESS THE MENTAL HEALTH PROBLEMS OF CHILDREN, CALL OR WRITE:

THE CENTER FOR APPLIED PSYCHOLOGY, INC.
P.O. BOX 61586
KING OF PRUSSIA, PA 19406
(800) 962-1141